THE
Egyptians

Ruth Thomson

Contents

3000 BC	2000 BC	1000 BC	0	1000 AD	2000 AD

Egyptians

Greeks

Romans

Vikings

CHILDRENS PRESS ®

CHICAGO

Who were the Egyptians?

The Egyptians lived along the Nile River. Most of Egypt was sandy, rocky desert. Every year, the Nile flooded the land on either side of it. When the water went down, it left behind a layer of thick, black soil. This was perfect for growing crops, so people always had food.

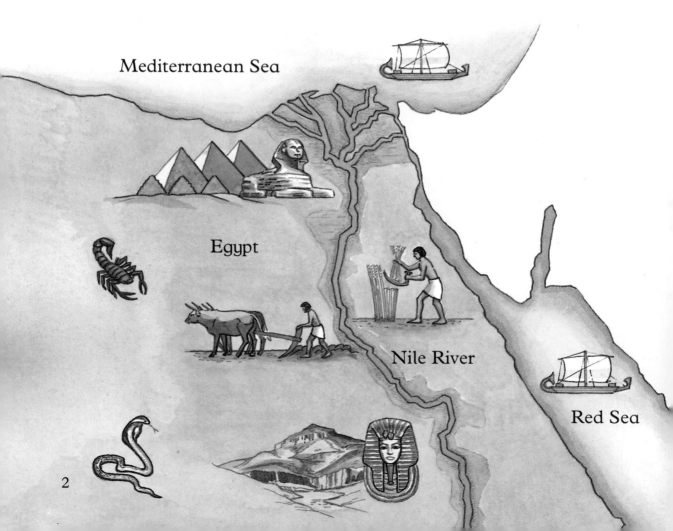

Mediterranean Sea

Egypt

Nile River

Red Sea

Ancient Egypt was ruled by a king called a pharaoh. He lived in a palace in a big city. Hundreds of officials carried out his orders. Writers, called scribes, kept records of crops and collected taxes. Potters, weavers, and other craftsmen made everyday things people needed. The poorest people were farmers and laborers.

A riverboat

Riverboats were made from papyrus reeds lashed together in long bundles.

You will need:

Corrugated cardboard	Pencil	Scissors
White glue	Paints	Paintbrush

Follow the steps . . .

1. Cut a strip of corrugated cardboard into the shape of a long leaf like this.

2. Cut four more strips the same size. Glue the strips on top of each other.

3. While the glue is wet, bend up the ends of the strips to make boat shapes.

4. When the glue has dried, paint your boat .

A collar necklace

You will need:

Large saucepan lid	White cardboard	Pencil
Scissors	Saucer	Paints

Follow the steps . . .

1. Trace the saucepan lid onto a piece of white cardboard. Cut it out.

2. Put a saucer in the middle of your circle. Trace the saucer to make a smaller circle. Cut

3. Cut a wedge from the outer circle to the inner one. Cut out the inner circle. Try on your collar necklace. Cut a bigger hole if it does not fit you.

4. Fingerpaint jewels on your collar necklace with bright paints.

7

Homes

Houses in ancient Egypt were built of mud-and-straw bricks, baked hard in the sun. Their thick walls and small windows kept out the heat of the sun. The houses of rich people had many rooms with wall paintings and tiled floors. They also had large gardens with pools.

But the houses of most people had only a few rooms, with whitewashed walls and a dirt floor. People had very little furniture. They slept on wooden beds, kept clothes in chests, and stored their food in clay jars. People often cooked and slept under a cloth canopy on the flat roof.

A model house

You will need:

Modeling tools   Clay   Board   Knife

Follow the steps . . .

1. Flatten some clay on the board. Cut it into an oval for a courtyard.

2. Put a big lump of clay at one end of the courtyard. Shape it into a house. Carve some steps and hollow out the inside.

3. Roll a flat wall out of clay. Cut it out. Join it to the front of the house. Cut out a window. Add an arched door.

4. Make a low wall out of clay.
   Place it around the courtyard.

A painted chest

Houses had very little furniture. People sat on stools or cushions. They stored their clothes and tools in chests.

You will need:

Shoe box with cover	Pencil	Scissors
Cardboard	Paints	Glue
Paintbrush		

Follow the steps . . .

1. Paint the shoe box and the cover.

2. Cut out four pieces of cardboard for legs. Roll them into tubes and glue. Paint the legs and let them dry.

3. Cut into the ends of the legs. Open them out. Glue one leg to each corner of the box.

4. Cut four small circles of cardboard. Glue one to the other end of each leg.

13

The Pharaoh

The pharaoh was the ruler of Egypt. The people also believed he was a god on earth and that he had the powers of a god.

The pharaoh was the head of the government, the army, and the courts of law. He was the chief priest of the temples. He owned all the granaries where food was stored.

Thousands of officials carried out the pharaoh's orders. The most important official was called the *vizier*. Wealthy nobles were in charge of the water supply, the granaries, and tax collecting. The Egyptians did not use money. People paid taxes with crops or other goods, or they worked on the pharaoh's building projects.

Writing with pictures

A

B

C

D

E

F

G

H

I

J

K

L

M

N

O

P

Q

R

S

T

U

V

W

X

Y

Z

CARTOUCHE

The Egyptian language was written in pictures. This kind of writing is called *hieroglyphics*. Each character is called a *hieroglyph*. Sometimes the pictures meant exactly what they showed. The same pictures also could stand for one or two letters. The pharaoh's name was always written inside an oval border called a *cartouche*.

You will need:

Paper   Felt-tip pens

Follow the steps . . .

1. See how many *hieroglyphs* you can learn to write.

2. Use the *hieroglyphs* to write your name inside a cartouche.

The Pyramids

Some of the first pharaohs had enormous tombs, called pyramids, built for them. They were built from stone blocks. Some are still standing today.

The Egyptians believed that when people died they went to a new world. People filled tombs with clothes, food, furniture, jewels, and clay figures of servants. They thought the dead would need these things to make their new life comfortable.

Artists painted scenes on the inside of the tomb. These showed the life people hoped to have in their new world after death.

The pharaohs' pyramids held such great treasures that robbers tried to steal from them. Later pharaohs built tombs underground with mazelike corridors to secret burial chambers.

A mummy

The Egyptians believed a dead person would need his body in another life. To keep it from rotting in the tomb, they took out the insides, dried the body, and wrapped it in linen bandages. Then the body is called a mummy.

You will need:

Cardboard tube	Scissors	Newspaper	White glue
Adhesive tape	Paint	Cardboard	Stone

Follow the steps . . .

1. Push a ball of newspaper into the tube for the head. Fold strips of newspaper for the arms.
Tape them onto the tube.

2. Put a stone in the tube. Cover the end with cardboard. Add newspaper feet.

3. Wrap the mummy in newspaper strips dipped in glue. Leave it to dry. Paint it.

A scarab amulet

An amulet was a charm that the Egyptians believed would protect them against evil. Amulets were worn, or buried with mummies, to ward off evil spirits. The *scarab* (beetle) was the symbol of the most important Egyptian god – the sun god.

You will need:

Modeling clay   Modeling tool or blunt pencil

Follow the steps . . .

1. Shape the clay into an oval dome shape.

2. Model the shape of the head and the body of the scarab.

3. Carve a pattern on the scarab's back using a blunt pencil or modeling tool.

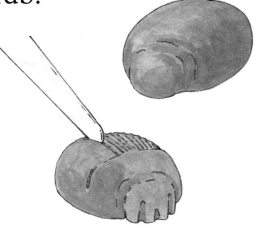

23

INDEX

Entries in *italics* are activity pages.

1995 Childrens Press Edition
© 1995 Watts Books, London, New York, Sydney
All rights reserved. Printed in Malaysia.
Published simultaneously in Canada.
1 2 3 4 5 R 99 98 97 96 95 94

Series Editor: Annabel Martin
Consultant: Richard Tames
Design: Mike Davis
Artwork: Cilla Eurich and Ruth Levy
Photographs: Peter Millard

Library of Congress Cataloging-in-Publication Data:

Thomson, Ruth.
    The Egyptians/ by Ruth Thomson ; illustrated by
Cilla Eurich and Ruth Levy.
    p. cm. – (Footsteps in Time)
    ISBN 0-516-08056-3
    1. Egypt–Civilization–To 332 B.C.–Juvenile
literature. [1. Egypt–Civilization–To 332 B.C.
2. Handicraft.] I. Eurich, Cilla. ill. II. Levy,
Ruth, ill. III. Title. IV. Series
DT61.T48   1995   94-42231
932–dc20   CIP
                                               AC